PARENTHOOD

Also by John Elinger

That Sweet City: Visions of Oxford (with Katherine Shock)
That Mighty Heart: Visions of London (with Katherine Shock)
That Strange Necessity: Visons of Portmeirion (with Peter Honey)
The Seven Seas: Voyages in Verse and Colour (with Sandra Lello)
and
Marriage, A Sonnet Sequence (with Wendy Ball)

PARENTHOOD
A SONNET SEQUENCE

JOHN ELINGER
ILLUSTRATIONS BY PETER HONEY

SIGNAL BOOKS · Oxford

First published in 2023 by
Signal Books Limited
36 Minster Road
Oxford OX4 1LY
www.signalbooks.co.uk

© John Elinger, 2023
Illustrations © Peter Honey

A catalogue record for this book is available from the British Library.

ISBN 978-1-909930-96-4 Paper

Typesetting and cover design: Tora Kelly
Cover Image: Peter Honey
Illustrations: Peter Honey
Printed in the UK by 4edge Limited

FOREWORD

BY WENDY BALL

I WAS DELIGHTED WHEN MY HUSBAND (and partner-in-parenting) suggested that I might write the Foreword to this sequence of poems on Parenthood. It is a subject of the greatest importance, one we have thought a lot about, one we feel we have gained a good deal of experience of, learning much on the way, during the six decades since we began to create and gather our mixed and 'rainbow' family of three girls and three boys (two born to us, four adopted by us) in the early 1960s. The combined family draws on genes and forbears from more than half of the world's six inhabited continents! Nurturing our children, and providing continuing care for them (and *their* children, when they became adults) has been the great project of our lives. This is the book I wish we had been able to read before we began to form our own much-loved family.

We started young, marrying while still students at university in 1958, and our family was completed by 1970 – though, we fostered a seventh child for a time a year or two later to help a mother from overseas, who needed hospital treatment, when the Social Services were struggling to find experienced short-term carers. Her name was Ilsa, and she is still remembered with affection by the family, who quickly bonded with her and grieved to see her go. I admire foster-carers, though that is not our métier: we bond for life. John Bowlby was our guru, and I warmly support what the poet writes about the critical importance of maternal bonding and continuity of care in the early years, at least from birth to three.

So, I share his concern about the modern style (in the so-called 'developed world'!) of 'out-sourcing' childcare (sometimes before the baby has reached its first birthday); and I agree with his view that raising a family is ideally a task for two parents to undertake in partnership, while admiring those who seek, whether through choice or necessity, to do it successfully single-handed. Marriage helps, by cementing partnerships. And, of course, children (usually) help to cement marriages, too. He is also rightly critical of absent (or deserting) fathers, and reminds us of the evidence that the absence of a father correlates with, and is probably a significant cause of, educational failure, especially amongst boys.

Meanwhile, successive governments fail to provide financial help for young mothers who choose to stay at home to care for their babies − instead encouraging them to hurry back to join the work-force, as if the growth of the Gross National Product were more important to the health of a society than ensuring the best care for its children. In principle, the solution is surely simple: substantially increase Child Allowances for the first three years of a new baby's life, pay it to the mother, and encourage her to provide the full-time home-care that their babies want − and need.

These are clearly controversial and complex issues, but I urge readers not to focus on them to the detriment of reflecting on the positive messages contained within this sonnet sequence: for example, the importance of the acronym NESTLED (Nurture and Nutrition, Exercise and Enterprise, Stimulation and Sleep, Time, Talk and Tenderness, Love (defined as 'acceptance, care and trust') and Listening, the Environment at home (and outdoors), and Devotion to the parental 'Duty of Care'. This is the agenda for those who seek to be good (enough) parents. Notice the analysis of the 'seven stages' of parental care, from pre-conception to appropriate life-long care of adult children; and the idea of a scale of intensity, which alters over time, between hands-on responsibility for babies to the 'watching brief' for children who have matured into independent adults.

Tempora mutantur; et nos mutamur in illos. 'Times change, and we change as they do so.' Nonetheless, this account of the wisdom and insights we acquired in the active decades of our child-care (1960-90) and the lessons we have continued to learn with, and from, our adult children, may prove of value to succeeding generations. And please observe, and (I hope) enjoy the quality of the verse, which is designed to please, to teach, and to improve the lives of its readers. When I married my young husband, I thought I was marrying a poet! But, he became a scholar, teacher, adviser and leader (and the family's 'provider') over the course of the next half century or so, before taking up his creative pen once more – and proving me right! This volume is a companion-piece to the sonnet-sequence on the subject of Marriage, which he wrote to mark our Diamond Wedding. I warmly recommend them both!

INTRODUCTION

THIS BOOK IS A LABOUR OF LOVE, and the fulfilment of a commitment. I loved my own childhood – even though much of it was spent in wartime. And I also loved the years when our own children were growing up in our care – and, indeed, the several decades since then, when we have tried to learn the 'subtle skills' of caring for them as beloved adults. Parental care is lifelong. I have gradually come to realise that being a 'good enough parent' is the hardest challenge in life – and the most rewarding. These (annotated) poems summarise what I have learned: they are composed in gratitude to my own parents, wife and children (and my siblings and friends), who have been my mentors, and in the hope that they might help others who undertake the demanding role of parenthood.

They also contribute to the fulfilment of a commitment made when I wrote the RSA Report, *Start Right*, The Importance of Early Learning (1994), almost thirty years ago. The main thrust of that report was the critical importance of providing opportunities for good early learning by the establishment of high quality nursery education for all children aged 3-6 – which should represent the first stage of any decent national system of education. In that respect, while much has been achieved since 1994, much also remains to be done. We still need to learn from Finland! But our report also recognised the fundamental importance of the home and the parents, in partnership with the schools, and recommended a second study (and report), proposing that 'the RSA and other bodies should pursue the issues of: a) the education and support of parents, b) paid parental leave, and c) the care of pre-school children of those in employment (recommendation

11)' – see footnote xl at the end of this book. Sadly, I feel that there has been no adequate response to this recommendation. These poems are intended to re-ignite public concern, stimulate a national (indeed worldwide) debate, and persuade our governments and leaders to establish an enquiry – and act on its conclusions. When that happens, I shall submit this book in evidence.

Learning to be a 'good enough parent', and practising the skills of care, are lifelong challenges. I have found it helpful to think of the 'three dimensions' of good parenting: they are the seven *aspects* comprising the formula of NESTLED, the seven *stages* from pre-conception to the care of adult children, and the *range* of intensity from 'hands-on' to 'watching brief'. NESTLED stands for Nurture and Nutrition, Exercise and Enterprise, Sleep and Stimulation, Time, Talk and Tenderness, Love (defined as acceptance, care and trust) and Listening, Environment (the home and garden – or public park), and Devotion to the parental Duty of care. The sonnets explore and exemplify these dimensions and elements of a parent's role. Most of us learn to do much of this agenda well enough, but many fall short in adequate preparation (before conception); maternal care of the foetus in pregnancy (no alcohol!); continuity of care (and breast-feeding!) in the early years to establish attachment and bonding; fostering a healthy home-school partnership; providing time and talk (and, especially, patient listening!) with tenderness; and consistently offering a good role-model for our children (and grand-children!) throughout our lives.

When I wrote the *Start Right* report all those years ago, two paragraphs (5.8 and 5.9) disturbed a number of the members of my Advisory Committee, who insisted on their disagreement being recorded and included in the report (p.45). I have not changed my mind about the views expressed in those paragraphs, and have felt it right to reproduce them here. Readers will observe that the poems reflect these opinions. If they do no more than to re-ignite the controversy that they caused in

1994, they will have played their part in fostering the debate about what children want and need, and what makes a 'good enough' parent.

'5.8 The idea that parents are like professionals in having their own proper competence has important consequences. Like jurors or politicians, parents are ordinary people who undertake a task affecting the whole community. While not all parents can be expected to, or need to, follow one model of parenthood, parents who aspire to competence will seek exemplifications of best practice, wish to ponder the evidence of research, acquire appropriate education and training, and expect other professionals and the community as a whole to fulfil their responsibilities and provide support from the other two points of the triangle of care. These are controversial issues – so much so, that some members of the project's Advisory Committee wish to dissociate themselves from paragraphs 5.8 and 5.9. This report seeks to avoid two obvious pitfalls – common heresies expressed by the political left and right: namely, that the problems of contemporary parenthood can be resolved solely by better programmes of assistance (on the one hand), or by more responsible parenthood (on the other). Both are needed. It is not easy to present models of best practice without seeming to criticise those who (for whatever reason) do not, or cannot, conform to them. Some successful parents are non-conformists. But societies need norms, even though not everyone needs to observe them. This report does not criticise either single mothers, gay people, or separated parents. While it is probably true that it is poverty, rather than single parenthood, that is harmful to children, it is also true that poverty is more likely to be the consequence than the cause of single parenthood. In the present state of knowledge, there is a case, not so much for reasserting the traditional model of parenthood (with its pre-determined gender-specific roles), as for promoting a modern version of it (providing flexibility of role), with a mother and father who stay together at least until the (youngest) child reaches the age of parenthood, and who honour the contract.

5.9 Although this is a high ideal, increasing evidence suggests that two common alternatives are models which carry high risks for children, single parenthood and broken parenthood. We should not be surprised to discover that fathers are important for children's development and welfare, as well as mothers. Or that the stability of the home is a significant factor. Common-sense, as well as research, suggests that children (both boys and girls) need role-models of both sexes, that parenthood is quite difficult enough, even when two partners work together, to discourage those (who have a choice) from embarking on it alone, and that broken homes tend to be bad for children. Of course, there are many exceptions to these generalisations. And few people set out on the journey of parenthood with the intention of becoming single parents, or providing their children with a broken home. Most of those who start as parental partners intend to stay together. The advantages – for children and parents – of the collaborative model are obvious. Like jurors and politicians, parents need appropriate education and support; and like jurors and politicians, they don't always get it. One of the benefits provided by good pre-school education is the opportunity it gives for parents to learn and develop some of the skills needed for competence in the role. It is also important to ensure that personal and social education within the school curriculum provides a sound basis for competent parenthood. But more is undoubtedly needed: perhaps we should make available regular and systematic training for parents, possibly linked to the provision of child-benefit. The learning parents need is, of course (like most worthwhile learning), a complex mixture of knowledge, understanding, skill, experience, attitudes and values. Not all of what is needed to become a competent parent in a modern society comes naturally. Lastly, parents need the support of professionals (e.g. teachers, doctors, social workers...) and of the whole community. This is dealt with in what follows.' (Read the whole *Start Right* report. When it was published, it was headline news in *The Evening Standard*. And I recall, with wry amusement, an interview with a journalist who asked if I seriously expected parents to stay together until their youngest child reached the age of fifteen! 'No,' I replied, 'I was thinking of something more like thirty.')

The concerns I expressed then have not diminished; if anything, they have increased. But, rereading these paragraphs, I realise that something significant is missing: the critical importance of both continuity of care in the early years (0-3, but ideally 5), and the father's role thereafter. The sonnets address these issues, which are bound to be controversial (especially when the author is an old man!). Careful readers will note my concern that the growing prevalence of mental ill-health in childhood might (in part) be caused by failure to ensure continuity of care for babies. And they will also observe that I see some reasons to hope that the emerging practice of WFH (working from home) might partially alleviate the problem, and enable 'working mothers' to combine responsible parenthood with a rewarding (and inevitably demanding) career. Likewise, the correlation between absent fathers and educational failure. But, as I hope will become clear in what follows this Introduction, my concern is not primarily with the well-being and convenience of adults (neither fathers nor mothers), important as that most certainly is, but with the lives of children, who have few champions to speak for them, articulate their needs, and campaign for their cause. Above all, I hope these poems might help to make the modern world a better place for the young.

The poems are sonnets, formal verse in fourteen lines of decasyllables, with a variety of intricate rhyme schemes. I find the sonnet form an endlessly fascinating challenge. And I revere the great poets of the past, like Petrarch or Shakespeare, who were the masters of their craft. The ancients taught us that poetry should entertain, instruct, and help to improve things. Those are my aims: readers will judge how well I have responded to the challenge. I hope you enjoy them.

I gratefully acknowledge the support, help, and advice from my colleagues in our 'parenting project', Professor Pat Preedy and Dr. Jane James, whose expertise (and gender and relative youth) have provided a corrective influence from time to time. But I alone am responsible for what is written here. The exercise of writing these verses has led to several deep discussions. As in 1994, I should record that they have challenged some assertions, and disagreed with others – which makes us expect (indeed, hope for) a lively public debate after publication. I thank Dr. Peter Honey for the delightful illustrations. I owe a special debt of gratitude to Wendy, my wife during the last 65 years, for her generous Foreword, and leading role in what has been our life's mission, our family. (I chose well!) She has been an exemplary wife and mother. And I am also deeply grateful to the many members of our extended family and friends who have read these verses in draft, and responded to my invitation for comments. I asked them: 'What's missing? What is incorrect? And what is inappropriate?' (Their responses helped me improve the book.) Perhaps others will respond also; I hope so.

JOHN ELINGER (aka Christopher Ball)

PARENTHOOD

After they've learned the secret of survival,
all creatures seek to breed. We're just the same.
That's why we celebrate each fresh arrival,
and give the new-born child a home and name.
These two imperatives of evolution
(survival, procreation) govern life –
each one a challenge seeking a solution,
and each the source of trouble, grief and strife.
Making a living, raising children, both
demand commitment, skill and learning – though
the role of parents changes with the growth
of children, as experienced parents know.
This is a task for all our dwindling store
of fortitude and patience – and some more![i]

Compared with parenthood, survival is
the easy option, since earning a living
is hardly rocket science – unless his,
or her, career choice is the unforgiving
challenge of Astrophysics – while the role
of parent means a lifetime of commitment,
concern and care from hand, and heart, and soul
(We learned what 'others may, but we can't quit' meant.)
The parents are on duty seven days
a week, each week, and four and twenty hours
a day, throughout those early years. To raise
a child aright requires near-saintly powers.
Luckily, children are forgiving: they're
expecting 'good enough', not perfect, care.

I watched a nursing mother feed her child,
safe nestled in her arms and at her breast;
and wondered whether this might be the best
experience of our lives? – The baby smiled!
Consider: Nourishment and Nurture – is
it ever bettered? Sucking's Exercise
and Stimulation – sated now, she lies
aSleep. But I find further qualities
in what I saw – Time, Talk and Tenderness
suffused the scene; and Love – acceptance, care,
and trust; a safe Environment, for where
can we be safer, or life's peril less?
Remember NESTLED: D's devotion to
parental caring Duties – me, and you!*

---

* The word NESTLED recurs throughout this sequence
of sonnets: it is intended to remind the patient reader
both of the baby *nestled* in her mother's arms and at her
breast, and of the seven key aspects of good parenthood,
namely Nourishment & Nurture, Exercise & Enterprise,
Stimulation & Sleep, Time, Talk & Tenderness, Love
(defined as acceptance, care and trust) & Listening, the
Environment of family life (home & garden), and our
Devotion to our Duty of care.

What is the essence of good parenthood?
All complex subjects can be slimmed to three
key concepts: matter, energy, the speed
of light are what Physics is all about.
And Politics provides another good
example of 'the rule of three': the key
ideas are freedom, equity – you need
a third – community, without a doubt.
Good parenthood is best expressed by three
core qualities, *acceptance*, *care* and *trust*,
the key components of what's meant by love.
Whether from partners, parents – God above –
true love's found not in judgement, labour, lust,
but in love's *act*, good parents all agree.[ii]

Acceptance doesn't always mean approval.
Like adults, children err, and need correction.
We learn from our mistakes; but the reproval
should always show acceptance and affection.
Distinguish bad mistakes...from the dear person,
the wrong behaviour...from the darling child.
Never reject the sinner, lest you worsen
reproofs by failing to be reconciled.
Good parents in strong families select
acceptance as a default disposition.
All children thrive, secure in their belonging,
knowing they're loved – in spite of erring, wronging,
mischief in youth, with or without contrition,
and even crime. Good parents don't reject.

For home is where one's welcome – come what may.
So, make your home a safe and happy haven
of welcome for your children every day
throughout their lives – though they may misbehave and
transgress, from time to time. Love is the cure
for every ill, a moral penicillin
which parents need to keep in stock for sin
and vice in children (and each other!). Your
endurance may be tested – no one said
that parenthood is easy – but you must
accept, as well (of course) as care for, trust
and cherish, children you have jointly bred,
adopted, fostered...chosen to call yours.
The welcome of a loving home endures.

Care is the obvious one: good parents care
about and *for* their children all their lives –
whilst either parent, or each child, survives.
But child-care changes over time: compare
the infant, teenager and adult... where
the care-agenda alters: burping, breast –
essential for the baby – but the rest:
sex-education? tact? learning to care?
We learned parental care takes many forms:
nurture and exercise, sleep, stimulation,
time, talk, and tenderness, a good home where
the child finds welcome without reservation
from parents who, in sunlight or in storms,
display devotion to their task of care.

My mother taught me how to care: hot meals,
warm welcome, thoughtful questions, kindness were
what made our home a haven. We loved her.
Make your own home a place where each child feels
respected, cherished, cared for, special, loved...
each hour, each day, lifelong. Never take care
for granted; but take care to show and share
how much you care, so children feel beloved,
and learn the art of caring in their turn.
The world would be a better place, if more
of us had learned to care in childhood, for
(although it's not too late) it's hard to learn
to care in adult life. Good partners help, so choose
a mate who really cares for you – one not to lose!

———————

Trust is the hardest one. How do you trust
the untrustworthy child? Yet, everyone
betrays our trust from time to time, for none
succeed in always keeping faith. You must
learn to forgive an errant child; and just
renew your trust, for no one learns to be
trustworthy, if they are not trusted. He,
or she, will not grow straight, lamed by mistrust.
Parents lead by example – demonstrate
behaviour, disposition, feelings, thought
they hope to see their children emulate.
Our first role-models are our parents, who
once gave us life, shared genes with us, and brought
us up to follow in their footsteps, too.

But children mostly find their own way through
their lives – and parents have to trust them to.
Trusting the wilful infant's hard: but you
will find it's harder still to trust at all
the wayward teenager – hardest of all
is trusting adult children, when they fall...
in love, or in harm's way, perhaps become
addicted (gambling, drugs, self-harm, or some
variety of crime) – or just act dumb.
Love means acceptance, care and trust – so just
love them, regardless of their faults, in spite
of your lost hopes. When others can't, you must
continue giving children love. That's right:
love is the best medicine of all. (With trust!)

———————

The marathon of parenting comprises
 these seven stages: first, the planning; then
conception, pregnancy and birth (for some,
adoption); followed by the infant years,
the nursery phase – stage three and four; then come
the primary and secondary schools – when
the parents share their role with teachers. Wise is
the parent who remembers which one steers
the craft of childhood and child-rearing through
the school-years, puberty, to the last stage
of adulthood, for children look to *you*
for love – acceptance, care and trust – from birth,
in childhood, adult life, and as they age.
There is no limit to parental worth.*

———————

*   The *seven stages* of parenthood are here identified as the
     preparatory stage (before conception), pregnancy &
     birth, infancy (0-3), the nursery years (3-6), primary and
     secondary schooling, and our children's adulthood. These
     seven stages provide a second dimension to the *seven aspects*
     of parenthood set out above in sonnet 3, and summarised in
     the word NESTLED.

Distraction, chance, or choice mean many miss
the first stage altogether. Pregnancies
unplanned precede much ill-considered child-
rearing. Wise parents in the making take
their time to think about the family
they aim to raise, and practise two or three
segments of NESTLED (love, of course) and make
routines of nurture (say). Whatever's trialled
is learned well – Aristotle taught us this.*
Practise the *act* of love before the act
of sex which may conceive the child you mean
to raise, and plan the house and garden where
an infant can play happily and safe. Prepare
a home to satisfy a king or queen!

---

*   'What we learn to do, we learn by doing.'

The second stage of parenthood is nine
months long, on average: the pregnancy,
in some cultures, is counted as the first
year of a child's life – which, indeed, makes sense,
because these months matter so much to both
the mother's welfare and the child's health, growth
and well-being in future. Nourishment's
important: seek (and take) advice. (The worst[iii]
food's alcohol for foetuses.) The key
is love: accept, care, trust – all will be fine.
True love unknits the most entangled knots,
and care eradicates the darkest blots.
Both partners come to learn how best to share
devotion to this new duty of care.

Your child is born! Your life will never be
the same again. The NESTLED formula
provides a guide: feed, foster, cherish (Ma
and Pa) your precious flower. Experts agree
that 'breast is best' and 'nestled' at the breast
the babe will thrive and grow contentedly.
Trust midwives' lore: if parents fail to see
what *they* should do, *the baby* knows what's best!
Give time, and talk – with tenderness. Take care.
'Good mothers are for care,' wise children say –
then smiling add, 'And fathers are for play!'
Good parents make a complementary pair;
although they shouldn't strive to be the same.
Contrasting role-models should be their aim.[iv]

Not every family today is trad
(two parents, different sexes, Mum and Dad) –
though evolution and research suggest
(and children think so, too!) that trad is best.
Whether from choice or chance, a change of heart,
sadly, some partnerships just fall apart.
The single parent model is not rare,
though most have found the role requires a pair.
Same-sex parental partnerships provide
another pattern, but the child's denied
a close role-model of the other sex
(or gender) which may lead to side-effects
in adult life. Remember: parents give
us genes, raise us, and show us how to live...[v]

...and choose our schools. The nursery school comes first.
The nursery years (from three to six) provide
(or should) a sure foundation for our lives,
our learning, and our work. These years are when
we learn to learn; to read and count to ten –
but also skills, without which no one thrives:
commitment, focus, self-belief; the tried
and tested worth of practice, teamwork, thirst
for further learning. For, such 'subtle skills' –
even more valuable than rocket science,
or other 'hard skills' – are what guarantee
success in later learning: self-reliance,
strong families, the learning habit – three
conditions that protect us from life's ills.

———————

It's never premature to start to teach
a child about the facts of life and sex,
the differences between a girl and boy.
You need a language: we found 'front' and 'back
bottoms' sufficed, and bath-time's when
these things come up. Don't say too much; let each
child set the pace. The facts of life perplex
the young, who don't yet understand the joy
of sex, or reproduction. And they lack
sustained attention span (until they're ten
or more). Be patient: patience is a virtue
for parents, as for children – or they'll hurt you!
And don't forget that family is where
new lives begin, and flourish with good care.

And this is when a lasting partnership
needs to be formed between the home and school,
where common standards of behaviour rule,
and shared respect for kindness helps equip
the child for later life at school and home.
The NESTLED guide's for parents *and* for schools,
and takes its inspiration from the rules
taught by the Prophet and the Pope in Rome:
'Make peace, and feed my people.' 'Love creation,
and love your neighbour, as yourself.' These words*
are all we know, and all we need, to live
together, raise our children, free as birds,
with neither fear, nor war, nor altercation:
accept, care, trust; act kindly; give, forgive.

---

*   The founders of Islam, and of Christianity, provided us with
these noble ideals.

———————

A sense of wonder, gratitude and love
of nature are but three of several ways
of being we should help the child we raise
become familiar with. Names: duck or dove?
daisy or dandelion? Flowers (and pets)
provide a rich agenda on a walk
for questions, answers, explanations, talk
and learning. 'Why...? and how...?' No one forgets
those early lessons from a loving Dad
or Mum, who also teach us thankfulness
for meals and hugs and birthday gifts. (I bless
my parents for so much – for being glad
to be alive, for all those years of loving care,
that they were who they were, that they were always there...)

My sister says these sonnets have two gaps:
she calls them 'God and dog'! I think (perhaps)
she's right. Pets *are* important. We had cats:
they helped to teach our children care, and that's
a key part of the parents' role – as is
explaining how humanity's divided
between the faithful, those who have decided
there is a God (the ones who base their trust
upon the 'evidence of things not seen':
religions, with all their complexities) –
and those who don't, preferring to believe
what they can see. The third group, in between
these two, of course, are those who say 'I just
don't know'. Oh, what a tangled web we weave...

—————————

when first we practise to believe, or not!
Who's right? Who's wrong? In life, we can't be sure;
once dead, maybe all will at last be known.
The great thing is to teach our children how
to listen with respect, and then allow
the other's faith to differ from one's own,
or lack of faith. For tolerance can cure
more wrongs, than fierce beliefs, which rot
society and spoil our life on earth.
And, anyway, our actions count for more
than what we say: our thoughts (the third term!)* count
for even less: good deeds are paramount,
so, teach them kindness, and seek to ensure
they practise it. Kindness has lasting worth.

—————————

*   The 'third term' refers to my 'rule of three', see sonnet 4.

The rituals within a family
inform the science of ontology.*
All children's lives need patterns, duties, play.
Structure and shape, routines, define the day,
week, year, with birthdays, Christmas, the school terms,
and holidays. Each prized event confirms
the family security that each
child needs for comfort. Daily duties teach
the discipline of social give-and-take,
and offer opportunities to make
good habits which will last a lifetime. Play[vi]
is children's work, or so the wise ones say:
whether they play alone, together, or with you,
make time for play, whatever else you do.

---

*   Ontology: the science of being; the fundamental principles
    which govern the nature and essence of life.

Whilst competitive play is good (like Snap?),
imaginative play is better still
(Charades?); all forms of play develop skill,
though social games do more than any app,
or solitary play, to help a child
learn social skills – Grandmother's Footsteps, say
or Hide-and-Seek, or Hunt the Thimble. They
are games that make us mild – at least, less wild!
The digital epoch in which we live
today has changed the world, at home and work.
So, should we ration screen-time? The knee-jerk
reaction is, 'It can't be done!' But give
some thought to this: we raised our family
(in spite of protests!) in a home without TV...

...until the youngest reached the age of twelve.
After the nursery years a dozen years
of formal education (home or school?)
await the child: stage five and six of your
long parenthood – a role you cannot shelve.
After a trying school-day, what most cheers
your child is coming home, where one of you'll
always be there to greet them at the door.
This is when you must balance the demands
of earning, and child-rearing – nor forget
which one takes precedence: the child, of course!
Time, talk, and tenderness the internet
cannot provide. Nor love. Nor gentle hands
and biscuits. (Parents spend their lives in debt!) [v (again!)]

———————

Grand-parents help, of course – so, foster your
own parents, if you can. Both you and they
provide love unconditionally, but theirs
 is undemanding love, yours formative –
intent on child-development. They give,
without expecting a return. Your care's
inevitably purposeful. Each day
you nurture for the future. Be quite sure
you understand the difference: I call
them g-love, p-love. Grandparents are g-lovers,
parents must play the harder part as p-lovers.*
Together, they can give the children all
the loving care they need to thrive, and earn
success in learning, work, and life, in turn.

———————

*   'Glovers' offer soft love; 'plovers' provide tough love.

The years from nursery to puberty
can often seem in retrospect less hard
(not easy!) for the parents who are jarred
by infancy and puberty – when (we
now know) the brain and body both transform,
sometimes creating difficult behaviour
in children. Then, if parents need a saviour,
trust in time; sunlight follows every storm!
Meanwhile, enjoy the years at junior school,
when your child learns to read, write, calculate,
of course, but also 'soft skills': to create,
associate, interrelate, be cool –
and who he really is, and what she wants to know,
and how they like to learn, and where each aims to go.

Kipling's 'six honest serving-men' are all [vii]
you need – to learn, at school, in life, at work:
their names are *what* and *why*, and *when* and *where*,
and *how* and *who*. Children ask questions: they
are right! Encourage curiosity,
and help them find the answers that they seek.
(*Why*-questions are the hardest ones of all,
and sometimes make the parent go berserk!)
Recall that patience is a part of care –
a virtue parents need to find each day,
alongside fortitude. Questions can be
answered with questions: asked 'why does a week
have seven days?' a parent might reply:
'D'you think a shorter week would make time fly?'

We played a game called Real or Pretend,
and asked our children to decide which world –
of fact, or fiction – items each lived in:
stones, stories, angels, water, the week-end?
Asking good questions is a game wherein
a child and adult are on equal terms:
when thrown a question, our bright children hurled
one back! 'Are fairies real – or fear, or germs?'
Read to your children; let them read to you.
We asked our children each to choose an art,
a sport, a hobby (music, painting... football, gym...
drama or chess...) and filled their lives with new
activities and interests for him
or her to share, together or apart.[viii]

Help them with homework, but don't do it all
yourself. (I did – my daughter had to lie,
and never quite forgave herself, or my
mistake!)* The teachers are your friends: recall
the partnership agreement. Trust the school,
and trust the child. Strong families ensure
the young learn self-reliance long before
they're adults – since dependency's not cool,
and proves a liability as time
goes on, in learning, work and life. Support;
don't seek to manage or control. You court
disaster if you seek to halt the climb
to independent adulthood. 'Love me,
and let me go', they cry, 'I must be free.'

---

*   The teacher was Philip Pullman. Years later, we owned up.
    He forgave us.

Big school and puberty come next: each one
a trial for your child, and you. New friends,
new rules, and new routines... It never ends –
the challenge of life's changing patterns – none
more testing than their puberty, for girl
or boy. The facts are awkward, feelings more
disturbing still. Discuss them both – before,
during and after – the event: don't curl
up in embarrassment! The trials of
the parents multiply as children grow:
none worse than when a child dies, and you know
they cannot hear your voice, or feel your love.
Accept the loss, care for the memories,
and trust yourself to cope with blows like these.

School-life and home-life (both) seem challenging
for children now, coping with Physics and
the physicalities of sex, first-hand
experience of Biology, being
in love, wet dreams, embarrassment and shame.
They need your time (for talk) and tenderness:
you need to listen, not to second-guess
what they might say, for (by another name)
good listening's good therapy, like love.
Relationships are difficult – as well
as sex! Explain the rule of three, and tell
them to distinguish reproduction of
humanity, from orgasm, and each
from intimacy. Never preach, but teach!

Teach by example, stories and distinction:
just show, and tell, and separate...ask questions.
Sex saves a species (like ours) from extinction.
An orgasm needs skill – it's fun! – suggestions
of how to do it, found online, from friends,
in books, may help (or not); practice works best...
while intimacy, flower of love, transcends
all other aspects of human relations.
'Just learn to love...' the poet, Langland, taught,*
and you can cheerfully ignore the rest!
Love's evolution's summit and creation's
crowning achievement. (Sex is just a sport!)
Parents should help their children navigate
through puberty – and tell them what's what straight![ix]

---

*   'Lerne to love, and leve all other...' William Langland, *Piers Plowman.*

All social segregation's a mistake –
except in jails, and public loos, and sport...
Consider: men's clubs, (Women's Institute?)
apartheid, care homes, segregated schooling...
After reflection, we agreed to make
a home which mixed both sex and race: we thought
'the comprehensive principle' *sehr gut;**
likewise co-education. These were ruling
ideas for us – we frowned on 'privilege':
selective, private schools and boarding. Home
is where one's childhood should be spent – then roam
the world in adult life. Live on the edge,
if that's your choice, secure in your strong family,
with self-reliance, lifelong learning, brave and free!

*   Very good.

'So, what is education for?' you ask.
We used to answer: the three 'Esses': Skills,
Socialisation, Sorting. Schooling's task
is, first, the basic skills (three Rs) – those drills
(times tables, copy-books and spelling) – then
what seems like all of human knowledge: Greek,
Geography and Rocket Science... 'when
will we have learned it all? (It's French next week!)'
And all the time they're learning to behave,
and being tested, to ensure the good
ones get the best jobs (bad ones misbehave!),
preparing for their roles in adulthood.
School matters; learning matters. Partnership must rule
between the loving parents and the caring school.

Learning Matters–Timetable	
Mon	The 3Rs
Tue	Greek
Wed	Rocket Science
Thur	Behaviour
Fri	Preparing for Life

———————————

We used to ask our children to reflect:
what were they good at? then, what would they like
to do? and, lastly, what was needed most?
I hope it helped them thoughtfully select
their training and careers in business-like
fashion. The third question yielded a host
of good ideas: computing, caring, health,
(and fashion!) for example. And they each
found openings which led to work, and well-
being in well-lived lives, which brought them wealth
(enough, at least!) and satisfaction. Teach
children reflection and research. Don't tell
them what to choose: what worked for you is probably
now dead and gone (or moribund): things change, you see!

Explain the difference between a choice
and expectations. Choices – promises
we make ourselves – are special: if you voice
them, others help you dodge the miseries
of breaking undertakings. Expectations
are things that others may require of you:
consider, when they feel more like vexations,
whether they're fair and right – and proper, too.
Our lives are governed by our choices, and
by others' expectations. Children learn
(or fail to learn!) how best to understand
the strong demands of either one and turn
to parents for assistance – who must seek to give
both explanation, and example, how to live.

Explain how natural instincts govern life:
above all else, the instincts to survive,
and procreate. The former's a strong drive
in every creature – children, man and wife,
a worm or wolf, an elephant or mouse.
But different instincts govern men, from those
we see in women, on whom life bestows
a natural 'nurture-habit' while their spouse,
a 'natural voyeur' will never cease
what seems an endless task of seeking mates,
while women always strive to lure new dates,
by looking like a picture by Matisse!
Our instincts govern us, while laws and cultures seek
to govern them: consider which is stronger, which is weak.

Then childhood ends, and adult life impends.
They start to leave the home (for college, work,
or travel) which becomes an empty nest.
But, as you grieve (or celebrate!) the rest
from parenting, you'll find the handiwork
(mind-work, heart-work) of parents never ends.
Following childhood, education, there's
a third novennium* I call *formation*.ˣ
(The adult brain is still developing
throughout the third decade.) You need to bring
your *'nestled'* skills to help for the duration –
and not just cash, concern, a bed... For care's
not only meals and money. A true friend
is what you seek to be, until the end.

---
*   A novennium is a period of nine years.

I took each of our children on a walk
(a long one!) when they reached the age of thirty.
This gave us both some time to have a talk,
as bones began to ache, and boots got dirty –
and listen. I suggested they might need
to tell me where I'd failed them as a father,
lest past resentments last, which might impede
the adult friendship we should share now – rather
than the old parent-child relationship.
Perhaps this helped us both move on and grow
into a new phase of our lives, and strip
away impediments from long ago.
(Of course, there'll come a day, at our lives' end,
when *they'll* be caring for *us*, as *our* friend.)

As adults, children live their own lives, make
their own decisions (and mistakes, of course).
Alongside patience, you now need restraint –
from interference, offering advice
(unasked) and 'knowing best'. Give tea and cake,
or tea and sympathy, but never force
your hard-won wisdom (or voice a complaint!)...
Silence is golden* – and it must suffice.
And this is doubly true, once you become
grandparents, and desire to share your skills
with those (and for those) whom you dearly love.
Now most of all must you choose to stay dumb,
since unsolicited instruction kills
relationship, when push can come to shove!

---

*   *Sprechen ist silbern, schweigen giltern.* 'Speech is silver; silence
    – golden.' Thomas Carlyle, *Sartor Resartus*, quoting a Swiss
    inscription.

Let *nestled* be your guide. My mother thought
she ought to feed us well, and liked to walk
with me – when, as she listened, I would talk.
She asked good questions, offered her support,
and gave her time, her tenderness, and care;
helped in our home, but never interfered
as we learned 'parent skills' in turn, but cheered
us on: whenever needed, she was there.
She understood the D which means devotion,
and practised faithfully her caring duty
which constitutes parental truth (and beauty).
Remembered now by all with warm emotion,
she was a model parent, and an inspiration
to each of us, who sought to follow her vocation.

Nurture and nourishment come first in *nestled*.
(You may imagine how I must have wrestled
with rhyme and meter, making these lines scan.
Sonnets are hard: you do the best you can!)
Nurture means helping living things to grow
and thrive, while nourishment's good food. I know
they seem alike, but parents need to give
them both due weight if children are to live
good lives in health – and wealth, and happiness.
Apart from mother's milk, their diet should
be plant-based and unprocessed meals – a good
regime for all of us (but I digress).[xi]
Beware of dairy, meat and sugar; try to feed
your family, not what they want – but what they need.

Nature is given, nurture's what you give
your children in their childhood, when they live
at home and look to you for all they need:
security and sustenance, indeed –
but also exercise and interest.
Take them for walks (without your phone!) each day,
and notice what they see, hear what they say.
Encourage learning – which will prove the best
accomplishment they ever will attain.
The learning habit's one we should sustain
throughout our lives, alongside self-reliance –
more valuable skills than any science.
Strong families know this, and foster these
key qualities, the source of expertise.

Make sleep a routine – and a ritual.
Make bed-time fun! The bath: teach them to wash
'the seven places' (work them out!) and splash
each other. This should be a magical
event each day; dry them with love and soft
white towels... Don't forget to clean their teeth
(or see that they do). Make the bed beneath
them seem a bird to lift them up aloft
to slumber-land... tell stories; read a book;
and sing to them. Give time – show tenderness...
Turn out the light – 'Good night, Sweet sleep, God bless'.
Then leave the room without a backward look.
The secret of successful bedtimes comes
from ceremony, say experienced Mums!

Routines and rituals enhance a home.
(We marked the birthdays in our family
with flowers round the plate of birthday boys
and girls. Sundays were special in our home:
we cleaned the shoes, learned poems...) Family
customs like these remain with girls and boys
as they mature – pass on to generations
to come, as precious relics of good lives
lived well . (The walk on Christmas Day, New Year
and Bonfire Night...) These things link generations;
they're not forgotten; they enrich the lives
of young and old alike, for many a year.
Good customs make good families, I promise you:
remember yours with pride – create some new ones, too.

Good parents stimulate their children: try
to interest them every day, but not
over-excite, or frighten them, for what
they will remember by and by
are good surprises – kittens, holidays,
birthdays and celebrations, pantomimes,
the theatre, games and sport, the special times,
excursions and adventures, happy days...
Family meals, three times a day around
the kitchen table, should be special, too:
events, where children reconnect with you,
and you with them; and time for talk is found –
and listening, and tenderness... Above
all else make meals a festival of love.

I calculate that in our family
some thirty thousand meals were made, and shared:
the breakfasts, lunches, suppers, all prepared
with care throughout the thirty years when we
were raising our six children, from the first
one's birth-day to the last one's graduation
to adult status. Parenthood's *vocation*:
neither a pastime nor a job – unversed
and unrehearsed, as most are, when they feel
the call to serve, for parents give a service
to others – and what we should observe is:
how hard they work to serve the Commonweal,
unpaid, untrained and undervalued. The world should
reward, and celebrate, and honour parenthood...

...when it's done well! Bad parenting does harm
to children – and society. That's why
I write these verses to exemplify
good practice, and perhaps equip and arm
new parents with the attitudes, the skills [xii]
and knowledge they will need for nurture
and child-care. For each parent is a searcher
for wisdom, doctrine, learning that instils
the competence their children crave and need.
This 'primer for new parents' might suggest
some ground-rules for the family: what's best,
what's bad... The *nestled* formula can lead
you in the right direction – and you must
remember love: acceptance, care, and trust.

And then it ends – and yet it never ends,
until you die, or they do. Children give
their parents immortality: we live
on in their genes and lives, for love transcends
the generations of a family,
and care is not forgotten, but creates
a rich investment which appreciates
through time. A parent's but a brief trustee
of the inheritance of good child-care
these poems celebrate, which children need,
which helps communities succeed,
which in a better world we all might share.
If this be error – but it's not, you know.
Just ask the young: they'll tell you it is so!

Most parents fail to plan a 'home agenda'
(unless they are the brave ones who home-school
their children): draft curricula of what
one hopes might guide them through life's complex maze.
The Ten Commandments: parents might well spend a
spare hour or two discussing what each rule
might mean today: most start with 'Thou shalt not...'
(do bad things), but some teach us all to praise,
love, honour, value...what is good and true.
Or the Five Practices of Islam: give,
study, reflect, fasting and pilgrimage –
a discipline to show us how to live.
Or talk about the things we humans need to do
to guard our health, be happy, earn a living wage.

———————

Before they leave the kind cocoon of care
good homes provide, one hopes that children learn
three lessons, each essential for success
in learning, work and life: integrity,
and competence, and leadership. The first
means making promises – and keeping them!
The second's getting things – the right things – done.
The third means *realising*, both in word
and deed (demeanour too) the vision shared
by all participants – making it live
by living it. For nothing works without
good leaders, competence, integrity.
Good parents' lives exemplify these three,
transforming life's dull prose to poesy.

Perhaps you might discuss the paradox
of kindness – and 'the rules'. The human need
for order leads to laws and rules, for we'd
be lost without them. No one thoughtful mocks
the rule of law, ethics, or courtesy.
All children ought to learn to keep the rules,
both in the home and at their several schools.
We also need to learn how we may be
thoughtful and kind, forgiving, gentle, too,
with those who break the rules, do wrong, and choose
what's not allowed. It's never right to lose
the art of love, whatever others do.
Hurt feelings often make us less than kind. Discuss
whether we choose our feelings – or do they choose us?

Your choice

Share knowledge – and share skills, like how to clean
one's teeth, and fingernails, the bath, or stairs.
Learning to use the toilet on one's own
before school-age should be practised at home.
Teach them to cook, make their own beds, routine
responsibilities of care, for care's
essential for the well-lived life, alone
or shared, the care of self and others, home
and garden, pets and toys, the neighbourhood...
While skills and knowledge matter, *attitude*
is most important. The 'marshmallow test'[xiii]
(we offered Smarties) can provide a good
(and happy) way to learn life's lessons: you'd
teach them deferred delight is often best...

...and trusting (sometimes) is a risk worth taking.
Later, you might tell them about Maslow's[xiv]
instructive pyramid of human needs:
the body's needs come first, and form the base –
breath, water, food, warmth, shelter (and some clothing!);
above, our safety, health, asleep or waking;
on the third level (if you want to know)
come love and home, without which none succeeds;
still higher, you will find the special grace
of self-respect (none thrive, who learn self-loathing);
'self-actualisation' forms the crest:
meaning and mission make a good life blest.
(Those mindful of well-being know the 'rule of five':[xv]
connect, be active, and aware, keep learning, give.)

As they grow older, you might well discuss
the interplay of human nature (genes)
with nurture, both at home and school, which means
so much to how our lives work out for us.
While evolution has (for better or
for worse) determined how we are and what
we do (survive, and procreate), a lot
remains that culture's answerable for.
Invite them to consider how much they
do what they always do – Habitual
behaviour; how often they do what all
the rest are doing – Herd behaviour, say;
how readily they search for the next 'High' – [xvi]
a chocolate, or a chip! (And ask them why.)

This list of '(H)aitches' might remind us how,
conditioned by our culture and our genes,
we tend to overlook the third term: choice!
Germs can't make choices: humans can, and must
do all they may to learn the skills of choosing
wisely, in action, thought and speech, both now
and in the future. Tell them that this means
learning how to ignore the siren voice
of crowds, resist bad habits, and mistrust
temptation – even if this means they're losing
some friends, perhaps, some pleasures, and their guide –
that faulty autopilot of our lives,
called habit. (A kind marriage helps, we find, where wives
coach husbands, husbands wives, till each is satisfied.)

Of course, the early learning of a child
happens at home: learning to walk and talk,
say 'please' and 'thank you', manners, gratitude,
bonding and tidiness – obedience, love;
rebelling – and becoming reconciled;
using a spoon, and then a knife and fork,
at meals; the tastes of known and novel food;
waiting your turn, and learning not to shove,
laughter and sorrow, parties, loneliness...
the list is endless! People say that all
you need for life you learn in nursery:
I learned it all at home, and often bless
my parents, who (I guess) thought me too small
for school till I was six. (When I was *me!*)

There is a third dimension to the model
of parenthood set out in these verse-lines.
Beside the seven skill-sets summarised
in 'nestled', and the seven stages parents learn
to navigate, as children grow and age,
I find a third 'scale of intensity' –
unless the idea seems to you pure twaddle!
From 'leading role' to 'watching brief', this cline's
the map of progress to the highly prized
virtue of self-reliance – children earn
their freedom from parental care – each stage
a struggle for responsibility,
which they must win, and you will lose one day,
when they pack up their things, and go away.

Leaving a child to forage for its food
would be absurd: we'd think it gross neglect!
But think about the children who expect
a car or flat, for free! Parents delude
themselves, and spoil their young (I mean it!) by
depriving children of the privilege
of adult self-reliance. Parentage
that just prolongs dependence goes awry.
Appropriate 'intensity' at each
stage, for each element, is requisite:
time, talk and tenderness, and love, permit
no slackening, but what these verses teach
is this: good parents constantly review their role,
and seek to shape it into one coherent whole.

Always consult, and never undermine
each other in performance of child-care.
Make rules together – and all will be fine.
Jointly decide on diet, bed-times, where
to go on holiday, and when they must
be home, allowances and pocket-money...
Be sure you still deserve their lifelong trust –
for children, warring parents don't seem funny.
Remember Wordsworth's words, who wrote of 'that[xvii]
best portion' of good people's lives (it reads)
'those little nameless unremembered' deeds
'of kindness, and of love'. *Sic floreat*
*parens.** The ritual of *nestled* can ensure
that families grow strong, and partnerships endure.

---

* 'And so a parent blossoms'.

Great riches, when inherited, do harm
(so often) that good parents in old age
with wealth to leave give thought to this, and gauge
how much – to let them die without a qualm
of worry – will suffice in legacies
for their grown children, leaving what remains
to charity. We have. For what sustains
relationships is love, not money – is
not wealth, but care and kindness. (Once, aged ten,
our grandson told us we should leave it to
the younger generation, like him, who
had rather less than their rich parents – then!)*
I love the wisdom of the young, and guess
we ought to listen more – and lecture less!

---

* But I'm glad to say that he is now earning a good deal more
   than I ever did!

And then, at last, you grow so old, it's you
who need your children's care. Grow old with grace,
and let their caring seem a privilege,
and not a burden for them. Patience and
good humour, you'll discover, are but two
parental virtues you need to embrace
(again!) in this last stage of parentage –
I watched my mother die, holding her hand,
smiling as I recalled she'd let me go
at birth, as I bid her farewell in death –
and fortitude, of course. For this I know:
both child and parent, till that final breath,
are bound together by the *nestled* guide – above
all else, by the acceptance, care and trust of love.

I asked both friends and family to read
the first half-century of sonnets on
the theme of parenthood. (And they replied!)
'What's wrong? What's missing?' I enquired, 'And what
seems inappropriate?' There's no great need
to change what I have so far worked upon
(to my relief!). They called it 'a good guide' –
but felt that more was needed (true!), and not
all topics were sufficiently p.c.
(To some, the fifteenth sonnet seemed unwise,[xviii]
or just unfortunate?). Bereavement, guilt,
sibling relationship – these are but three
good topics to address, as I revise,
expand, and add new themes (before I wilt!).

A child, who dies before their parents, leaves
a lasting scar on all the family
who share the loss. Today, this tragedy
is rarer than it was: no one believes
it might happen to them, and when it comes,
we're ill-prepared for grief, and have to learn
hard lessons our grand-parents, when their turn
for grief arrived, already knew: grief numbs
the mind, and though time heals – in time – in part,
it never leaves you. You must learn to live
with loss, give thanks for ones you lose, forgive
whatever needs forgiveness, while your heart,
like that poor Wedding Guest's who 'rose the morrow morn',[xix]
feels sadder, yes, but wiser, too – and not forlorn.

'We blame the parents!' – we would say, and smile,
when things went wrong, or children misbehaved.
For parenthood is hard, like most worthwhile
commitments: marriage, physics, verse... (I've slaved
to make these sonnets work in form and meaning!)
It's surely true that parents, who supplied
our genes, then *nestled* us through childhood – weaning
and schooling, puberty and uni – guide
(for better or for worse) the growing child
a good deal more than others (carers, teachers,
siblings or friends...). In adulthood, we're mild
(or wild!) because we are our parents' creatures.
But parents are not perfect. No one is. We do
the best we can, and hope our kids will, too.

While self-reflection is a virtue, self-
reproach is not! And guilt (unshriven)'s worse.
Reflect – and learn. One should not judge oneself.
(Leave that to others!) Faced with a reverse,
an errant child, your own mistake, a loss...
do not seek refuge in regret, or guilt
(which solve no problems, and cause one to wilt
still more, like him who killed an albatross
in Coleridge's poem), but take time,[xix (again!)]
take stock, responsibly clear up the mess,
and start again to be a parent – less
judgemental, maybe, more forgiving... (I'm
still working on it!) For the parent's role is one
where learning's still required, until our lives are done.

———————

Our siblings help to shape us, both as kids
and 'groans' (as we kids called our parents once!).
My sister and my brother shared the stunts
and stories of our childhood: what we did's
forgotten now, but helped to shape our lives.
I thank them. Siblings are role-models, too.
They help to civilize and nurture you,
and, if we choose good husbands and good wives,
we owe them (with our parents) a great debt
of gratitude. As eldest, I enjoyed
my years as 'only child', but would avoid
that role, if I am born again and get
to choose! Today, each sibling is whom I depend
upon for insight, guidance... as a faithful friend.

'Are girls and boys so different?' asks my friend.
Strange question – controversial nowadays!
But parents always find they have to raise
the sexes differently: they often tend
(unconsciously, perhaps) to raise females
for motherhood, as much as earning money,
once thought a largely male preserve. It's funny
to see how evolution countervails
the cultural imperative for fairness.
And parenting's the battleground for this
debate – but, lest I fall into the abyss
of 'non-p.c.-dom' (or of unawareness),
I'd raise all children to be self-reliant earners –
good parents, also – but, above all, lifelong learners.

———————

Survival, procreation, are the two
imperatives of evolution. Where
on earth's the 'third term' that might prove to you
my 'rule of three'? It's culture – premiere
achievement of our species: arts and sport,
religions, rituals, the sciences,
philosophy and language. We have wrought
a complex way of being, one which is
a challenge for the parents to pass on
to children, since it changes constantly,
though gradually. (While semaphore has gone,
perhaps, the internet still puzzles me!)
Parents show children how to navigate
our culture, as its elements mutate.

And children teach their parents, too, for all
too easily we adults can become
frozen in time. The world may change, but some
of us find adaptation not at all
a simple task, and children (and grand-kids!),
the ones who've learned to learn, can learn to teach
their elders *dos* and *don'ts*, in place of *dids*
and *didn'ts* now no longer apt in speech
or thought or action. Parents make mistakes
sometimes, like babies: and their children may
bring them up short, correct them... and that makes
me think, in short, that sometimes it is they
who bring us up! Humility is yet
another virtue parents need to get.

Especially high-achieving parents, who
can sometimes seem to overshadow their
poor sons and daughters: failure threatens, where
the expectations seem too high for you.
(Just learn to love...) And inconsistency
in parenting should be avoided, you
should keep your word, support each other, do
what you have promised, never disagree
with one another (save in private!); or
be tempted by the 'good cop/bad cop' game.
The rules and discipline should be the same,
whichever parent's laying down the law.
If this be error, and upon me proved* –
of course, it's not: from this I won't be moved!

---

*   William Shakespeare, Sonnet 116.

What if your parents weren't (quite) 'good enough'? –
asks a good friend – 'And what if death, neglect
or distance left your child deprived of grand-
parents.' Supply the deficit, and learn
the skills you need from better role-models.
It never is too late to learn's a lesson
for children *and* for parents (I confess an
attachment to proverbs and principles
like this!) No grand-parents? Why not just turn
to friends for substitutes? (Our dear step-grand-
kids chose us, and adopted us!). Respect
the children's wisdom, which proves good enough
to guide the parents, when they're at a loss –
unless they just demand more candyfloss!

Above all, don't be 'auto-parents', who
just replicate the practice of your own
forbears, for good or ill. Reflect, the two
of you together, for you're not alone
(I hope) – especially if you feel you might
be one of those astride the cycle of
family deprivation. (Yes, I write
these verses for *your* eyes, with care and love –
and hopefulness...). Remember the three terms
that start with H in sonnet 55:
resisting them (Herd, Habit, 'High') affirms
our adulthood, as long as we survive.
Our children need us to be grown-ups; otherwise,
all sorts of problems may (and many will) arise.

The stark truth is: good parents have good kids;
it's hard for children with bad parents to
become good citizens. What can we do
to help the struggling 'poorly-parenteds'?[xx]
Committed parents help each other learn
the skills and attitudes they need to raise
their children well. (And Home-Start helps.)* The maze
of guidance on the Internet might turn
you off – together with the piles of books
on parenting – but my advice is: read
these poems first (of course!) and then proceed
to google Bowlby (John). You're one who looks[xxi]
for more (the rule of three!)? *The Parenting
Puzzle's* one book whose praise I'm pleased to sing.[xxii]

---

*   Google Home-Start UK.

So, why is parenthood not trained for? Sport
and work, which matter less (and aren't so tough),
require some thorough training, where you're taught
the rules and skills, until you're good enough
to practise on your own. School's not the place
(nor time) to train the future parents: what
the schoolkids need's advice on how (just face
the facts!) safely not to have babies, not
how best to raise them, when they're ready. Fine
parental training's needed constantly
throughout the seven stages which combine
in the formation of one's family.
Ongoing training (ask Samaritans!) should be[xxiii]
compulsory for parents: him, her, you and me.

Of course, you'll say we learn it on the job
('sitting by Nellie', like apprenticeships).[xxiv]
Our babies do their best, but I'll not fob
you off by saying infancy equips
a child to be an expert in the art
of parenthood. I recommend the course
provided by Family Links, to start[xxv]
with, but you'll find you need to reinforce
the training, stage by stage. For lifelong learning's
the answer to all problems in this life –
health, wealth and happiness, family, earnings,
old age, marital or parental strife.
Just practise what you teach (the learning habit, in
strong families, with self-reliance.) Now begin!

During my lifetime I have seen a change
in patterns of child-rearing, which has meant
that many families out-source the care
of infants to day-nurseries today.
I wonder if this practice seems as strange
to you, as it appears to me? I went
to see a nursery in London where
three-month-old babies were enrolled – to stay
from 9.00 to 5.00, six days a week – to suit
parental 'working hours', I guess. I call
this model of child-care the 'kibbutz route',
and wonder if it suits the child at all?
For continuity of care's the key
to good child-rearing (0-5), you see.

In the developed world, economies
require that women join the work-force; and
the case that feminism argues is
another cause to help us understand
the reasons why the kibbutz model has
begun to supersede the home-based style,
although it doesn't work as well. Whereas,
both evolution and the infants smile,
when mothers raise their young at home,
at least from birth to three. As breast is best,
so home is where a baby feels most blest –
and evidence confirms this view. No tome
is written recommending that convenience
of parents should prevail. It just would not make sense!

For babies bond with mothers first, and then
quite slowly learn to bond with others, Dads
and siblings next, the home-based nanny (when
she is a long-term fixture): which all adds
support to the idea that far the most
important thing is continuity
of care throughout the early years. No post,
or role, job or responsibility,
compares with motherhood, the one we learn
to bond with first. A bosom friend, a spouse,
pets, grand-kids follow, but we rarely earn
or seek this precious link with those whose house
is not our own. Our bonding starts at home,
and stays there, wheresoever we may roam.

Bonding develops slowly, once the first is formed
(with mothers), at the rate of rarely more
than one each year in early childhood. Nor
is adult bonding fast: you've out-performed
the norm, if you can count more than a dozen
in a lifetime: your parents, siblings, kids,
your partner, close friends, (lover... tact forbids
further enquiry!); but not aunt or cousin,
work-mates, or 'Christmas-card-list' friends. Perhaps,
for some, their grand-parents and grand-children...
Bereavement is a test of bonding: one
still feels the loss, though years and years elapse,
when someone bonded dies. We learn the art
of bonding 'nestled' by our mother's heart.

———————

Which makes me wonder if the kibbutz-style
of child-rearing may be developing
a generation handicapped (you smile?)
by lack of early bonding: mothering
at home may be essential to our health
in later life. Bowlby was right: from birth
to three, as in the womb, the mother's wealth
(in a rewarding job) is hardly worth
comparison with what she can
(and ought to) give the child placed in her care:
remember 'nestled' (yes, I'm partisan!).
Secure within the mother's arms is where
the infant needs and wants to be:
and your baby knows best, believe you me!

But, lest you think I'm biased, fathers count
almost as much as mothers. Children need
both parents throughout childhood – and, indeed,
as adults. Absent fathers may account,
not just for poverty, but also failure
at school: the correlation's sadly clear.[xxvi]
Fatherless families often appear
to struggle: evidence should countervail your
desire to question it. Study the stats:
the best thing's marriage for the hopeful pair –
you'll find the strong cement's the vows you swear.
Those who desert a family are rats,
for nothing matters more than family.
Believe the children, if you don't trust me.

You may think I believe that all is lost
already, in the quest to foster better
parenting. Not at all! Though Covid cost
a lot – in lives and cash – we learned to set a
surer balance between the home and work
through WFH. (Good comes from ill:
the old rule never fails.) For telework
permits both parents, aided if you will
by home-carers, to give that quintessential
'nestling', with continuity of care.
Working from home will yield the evidential[xxvii]
basis to prove (or not) what I declare:
babies need Mums, for bonding and the breast;
children need fathers. Two parents are best.

It's also true that parents need the grace
of nurture (both in childhood and as adults)
if they're not to become those sad- and bad-ults,
these poems are intended to displace
with more committed nurturers, who 'nestle'
each other first, before the birth of kids,
during those precious years they live amidst
their children, and still later when they wrestle
with loss of purpose and an empty nest.
We all need the support in body, mind
and heart from those who love us. You will find
parental care of partners works the best:
time, talk and tenderness, of course. But, far above
all else, comes human kindness and the 'act' of love.[ii (again)]

If I could offer guidance to the unborn child,
I'd say to them, 'Just choose your parents carefully'.
Sadly, I can't – and nor can they. But he, or she,
can seek to cherish, care for, become reconciled
with, those that nature (or adoption) gave to them.
'Honour and love your parents...' is Commandment 5;
the Bible says, '...you'll live a long and happy life'.
To children, mother, father, siblings, husband, wife
I say, 'Just love and cherish family, and thrive'.
A loving, happy family's a precious gem:
'infinite riches in a little room' are found
in homes where kids and parents live in harmony
and love [acceptance, care and trust], and peace profound.
The secret is to share responsibility.

Some parents raise large families. (We did.)
Some small. The choice is yours. Think hard and long
before you start the third, or further, kid.
All families are major projects: wrong
decisions about size of family
may hurt you all: economies of scale
apply with clothes and toys, but not with key
components of the 'nestled' list: you fail
as parents if you don't give all your love
to every child – acceptance, care and trust,
with time, and talk, and tenderness; above
all, maybe, patient listening's a must.
You might think China's two-child policy makes sense –
since two still prove a test of parents' competence.

And some, the parents of a pair of twins
(or triplets – maybe quads, or even quins!)
find nature's granted them a good deal more
to cherish than they'd really bargained for.
Multiple births provide a challenge *and*
an opportunity, for, on one hand,
while twins mean twice your heavy task of care
(to 'top and tail', and so on) – don't despair:
they bonded in the womb, and loved each other
some months before they even met their mother!
You'll find, from birth to death, they'll seek to share
with you, in partnership, the task of care.
Multiple births are truly blessings in disguise:
few parents granted them would wish it otherwise.

But what about (you ask) the 'only child'?
So what's the problem? Many make it work.
Some choose to be, some nature chooses, who
create and raise just one. (Adoption might
provide an option? Not for all.) Ensure
the friends and family (the cousins?) give
your 'only' sibling-substitutes. Though mild
or wild they may be, yet your 'master-work'
requires a peer-group (more than one or two)
to learn from, challenge, copy; see what's right,
what's wrong. For children learn to be secure
through life from parents, teachers, peers. (Forgive
me if I sometimes seem to say things twice or thrice:
we learn by repetition; once does not suffice!)

Our family of six, two 'born' and four
adopted, tested us, for sure! Adoption,
especially if delayed, we found, brings more
parental challenges. If that's your option,
remember 'continuity of care'.
Of course, it's better late than never; yet
we're sure these early months and years are where
we learn to bond, and when the habit's set.
So, if we could, we fostered them, before
adopting our dear younger ones, and sought
(while absent at the start) to miss no more
of *their* lives, and *our* duty of support.
The world needs more adopters. Children everywhere
grow up un-bonded, lacking good parental care.

Disabled children without parents are
the most in need, and often prove the most
demanding ones to raise. No fingerpost
or guide appeared, no sage, nor aide-mémoire,
when Peter, our fifth child was diagnosed
with Autism. We coped, and 'nestled' him
for thirty years at home (no kibbutzim!);
he loved his schools, played chess; his short life closed
in epileptic fit... He leaves a gap
(of course) and many happy memories.
He gave us more than we gave him, for his
condition proved to be no handicap –
instead, for parents, siblings, friends, above
all else, an opportunity for care and love.

———————

Children with 'special needs', like autism,[xxviii]
need special care: safeguarding first, of course,
respect (acceptance!), trust (come what may come!),
and patience... Parents readily endorse
what we have learned, that here's a role for all
one has of fortitude and patience. They,
above all, practise kindness – to the small
(and great!) responsibility (each day,
each night) entrusted to them – to each other –
and to themselves. Kindness, and love, and care
of wife and husband, father, child and mother,
provide the answers, and defeat despair.
For every child is special; every one of us
is special, singular, unique, and curious.

As generations pass, things change; the world
grows warmer, attitudes transform, our health
improves, our wealth increases, as – by stealth
or strategy – our future is unfurled...
And yet, the sum of human happiness
seems stalled; invention thrives in every sphere,
except society, since (everywhere)
the government of nations seems a mess,
and parenthood is patchy, at the best.
These poems have been written to set out
good practice, based on principles. No doubt,
some readers will demur, object, protest.
But if (at least) they stimulate informed debate,
they won't prove worthless. Challenges can educate.

The quality of government is bad;
the quality of parenthood is poor;
the quality of culture (the third term!) sad...
The future of the planet's insecure,
as man-made global warming threatens us –
and all life-forms. The ones who breed seem brave
(or foolhardy?) today. We must discuss
these issues with our children, since we gave
them life, and leave them to clear up our mess.[xxix]
Tell them the truth, and help them face the future:
what they deserve, and need, is nothing less
than total honesty. They may dispute your
suggestions: they'll respect sincerity.
Be their true model of integrity.

Our early years' experience shapes our lives,
the experts say. Our bodies, minds and hearts
develop most in early childhood. Five's
the age for full-time school, but growing starts
within the womb, and learning starts at birth.
Our parents are the ones who teach us how
to walk, and talk, and love – skills that are worth
a good deal more than rubies, and allow
the growing child to find success in life,
in learning, and (indeed) at work, in years
to come. Mother and father (husband, wife)
may launch a life of smiles, or one of tears.
No one at all is more important to us than
our parents, who will influence our whole life's span.

So, never cease to love and care for these
you choose to raise, who form your family.
Nothing should matter more to you (and me)
throughout our lives than these, whether they please,
perplex, or trouble us – the ones who share
our homes, and lives, the ones we've 'nestled', our
life's work, our children, through those sweet-and-sour
decades of hope and trust... (Never despair!)
I love to witness good examples of
parents at home, devoted to their duty
of care – a joyful sight, a thing of beauty,
which represents the true meaning of love.
Honour all mothers and all fathers, those
who love, and care, and trust, till their lives close.

To raise a child aright's a task requiring
'support from a whole village'*, not just two
parents – or only one, sometimes – as you
will find. Parental care's intense, more tiring
than any other work, and often hard
to comprehend and master. Study, read,
reflect, and take advice. All parents need
support; and few of us survive unscarred!
So, guard your health and well-being, and care
for one another (and yourself) beside
your baby, lest it feels unsatisfied:
the deficit of care's felt everywhere.
More care (not extra cash) is what the world most needs:
A parent, whose priority is love, succeeds.[xxx]

Good parenting, the rule of three declares,
is love: acceptance, care and trust. Now learn
the formula of 'nestled': practise it.
Recall the seven stages, and the scale
of apt intensity... This framework bears
the weight of most of what will most concern
new parents, and practitioners. Permit
me to repeat key points where parents fail:
in careful preparation, nourishment
in pregnancy, and bonding after birth,
ensuring continuity of care.
The home-school partnership; a 'firm-but-fair'
routine and style, agreed by all, are worth
adopting, and keep families content.

And don't forget another 'rule of three':
the learning habit, self-reliance, and
the strong, safe haven of the family.
Wise parents know what works; they understand
that children need *both* refuge in the home,
and independent freedom to create
their own lives their own way, explore and roam,
find new experiences, fresh fields; migrate,
perhaps; and leave the world you know behind.
When our children surprise us, we should not
be too surprised! (And certainly not mind.)
Remember that the baby in the cot
is yours in trust for just a few short years, before
she leaves home, goes his own sweet way, is yours no more.

That said, for now, this sonnet-sequence ends.
There may be more to come, my patient friends –
for what I've missed, or marred, I'll make amends.
(I hope that nothing that I've said offends.)
The subject is too serious to spoil
and, though I've had to burn some midnight oil,
for verse requires both artifice and toil,
I hope these seeds will fall on fertile soil.
I send good wishes to new parents who
(like us) set out to raise a child with few
(if any) clear instructions what to do
(or not)... Be kind, be brave, be patient, through
the joys and sorrows, days and years (and doubts!) to come:
there are no roles more valuable than Dad, and Mum.

And so my ton of sonnets seems at last
complete. I may write more – and likely shall,
but in a future year, and different form.
I wish I'd known, those several decades past,
what I have learnt, and share: the critical
importance of correct parental care.
These verses seek to guide you to conform
to no set *pattern*, but to *principles*
which all good parents illustrate, and share:
the NESTLED formula, with basinfuls
of *love* (acceptance, care and trust) and *time* –
each day for children, lifelong once they're grown.
These words may prove good guides, once known,
and understood, and practised. (Trust my rhyme!)[xxxi]

NOTES

i   Robert Louis Stevenson, musing on family life in an essay entitled *A Christmas Sermon*, wrote, 'Here is a task for all that a man has of fortitude and delicacy...' I have adapted his words, having discovered that patience is even more important (and much more difficult!) than delicacy. It was one of my mother's favourite quotations. (Mothers, of course, are nature's saints!)

ii   These poems celebrate the qualities of love and the nature of loving (rather than the feelings of 'being in love') and they are summarised in the word *act*: Acceptance, Care and Trust.

iii   It is now clear that good nutrition, both before and during pregnancy, is critically important for both the mother and her baby, before and after the birth. Seek advice, and take it!

iv   Children are more instinctive creatures than their parents, whose instincts have been controlled, adapted, and altered by their own childhood and education, not least by the prevailing culture they gradually acquire, including ideas of 'political correctness'. Humans are a mammalian species, and other mammals, like cats or sheep or elephants, remind us that we belong to a class of animals that suckle their young. Mammalian males are typically combative, competitive and curious; the females are conjugal, caring and careful. Testosterone shapes male behaviour, just as oestrogen endows females. Children instinctively cleave to their mothers in the early years, and they seem to need the full-time presence of the mother between birth and the age of three (at least). They are right to do so, and we must adapt our arrangements for parental leave to ensure that the period of 'attachment and bonding' is not foreshortened. This is a matter of great importance since it seems clear that early attachment and bonding over the first five years develops the conditions for social competence and emotional wellbeing. These will affect function at school and ability to build and sustain successful relationships throughout life. (I recall that a few weeks after the birth of our first child, we decided to go out one evening, engaged a baby-sitter and left the baby asleep. On our return, we found that the doctor had visited to see if all was well; he had left a note for us on a prescription form: it read 'Wot, no Mum?' As far as I can tell, cats and sheep don't have baby-sitters.)

v Some readers have been troubled by this sonnet, but I am unrepentant. These poems are intended to focus on what's best for the child, not what's convenient for parents. Recent decades have seen a major change in family life, as families move from the one-income model towards today's norm of both parents pursuing full-time demanding careers. I wonder whether this increase in family wealth has been accompanied by a reduction in family health? The second income is clearly desirable and convenient, enabling increased expenditure on housing, transport (the second car) and expensive holidays, amongst other things. Acton's Law teaches that 'Power tends to corrupt, and absolute power corrupts absolutely'. No tyrant has more absolute power over his people than parents have over their (younger) children. Of course, only a few grossly misuse it by practising child-abuse, but many might be guilty of child-neglect, who find excuses, in the form of arguments from convenience, for falling short in their duty of care. (Perhaps, I was one of them? I hope not.)

vi I warmly recommend the books by Sally Thomas on the subject of play and equipment for the early years: Familiar Things, Two Year Old (and Three Year Old) Best Practice Space, and her more general guide, Nurturing Babies & Children under Four. Play is a form of exercise (the first E of NESTLED) for both body and brain, whether the child plays games or music. (Each is important!) I also recommend the book edited by Pat Preedy and others (see note xxxi), especially chapters 3, 4 and 6, in this regard.

vii 'I keep six honest serving-men
(They taught me all I knew);
Their names are What and Why and When
And How and Where and Who.'
Rudyard Kipling, *Just So Stories* 'The Elephant's Child'

viii That said, it is probably a mistake to try to 'fill each unforgiving minute with sixty seconds worth of distance run' (Kipling) – in childhood. Children need space and time to reflect, become creative (on their own), and even to experience boredom – now and again. (The same, of course, is true for adults!)

ix Sex-education cannot (and should not) be left to the schools to teach: parents need to take responsibility to help their children understand, and learn to manage, the 'difficult' issues, like periods, masturbation, contraception, consent, and (above all) the complexity of sexual love. Fortunately, benign social change has gradually reduced the 'taboo nature' of these, and similar, issues. Progress is possible!

x A novennium is a period of nine years. The French word *formation* refers to the process of human development which follows education and precedes professional employment; the nearest English equivalent is 'training', but (like 'education') tends to be used to describe what is done to us, rather than our own growth and development, our *learning*.

xi A latecomer to the vegan diet, I have been persuaded by my grand-children that it is kinder to animals not to eat them (nor enslave them by animal husbandry), by the fact that it reduces global warming and the threat of climate change, and by Michael Greger (read his book, *How Not to Die*) that it is essential for our health and well-being. (Game, set and match to the vegans!) Of course, it might be *convenient* to continue a carnivorous diet, but convenience is a (convenient) excuse for unexamined habitual behaviour – which sets a bad example to our children. Socrates taught us that 'the unexamined life is not worth living'.

xii   Education is composed of knowledge, skills and attitudes. We used to call it the KSA curriculum. (I prefer the acronym ASK, because a positive learning *attitude* is essential for the development of *skills* like reading or numeracy – and, if you can read and calculate, the sum of human *knowledge* is available to you [in libraries and on the internet]. And the key to successful learning is to *ask* questions!) My 'rule of three' (Sonnet 4) claims that all complex subjects can be reduced to three core ideas: for example, the study of language comprises sounds, grammar and vocabulary. (The rest is detail!) Good teachers help learners to find their way into a new field of study by starting with the three core concepts, before indulging in the description of all the confusing (but, of course, for the teacher – delightful) details. Sadly, there are too few good teachers.

xiii   The marshmallow test was invented by Walter Mischel to measure children's readiness to delay gratification (and trust adults). The researcher places a marshmallow in front of the child and says that it is theirs to eat, if they want to; but that, if they wait for ten minutes, the researcher will return with a second marshmallow, and (provided the first one is still there, untouched!) the child may eat them both. The ability to delay gratification, and an attitude of trustfulness, in childhood seems to correlate with success in learning, work and life. Those who consistently 'fail' the test in childhood are sadly more likely to develop a drug habit, go to prison, or even to end their own lives in suicide.

xiv   Maslow's Hierarchy of Human Needs was developed by an American Psychologist, Abraham Maslow. It is shaped like a two-dimensional pyramid with five levels: the lowest contains our essential bodily needs (breath, water, food, sleep, etc.); above comes safety and security (including health); on the third level you find our need for love and belonging; higher still is where he places self-esteem (our confidence and self-respect); at the top is what he calls 'self-actualisation' – values, creativity, problem-solving, self-fulfilment, and poetry!

xv   The charity, *Mind*, recommends five ways to nurture our own well-being on a daily basis: connecting with friends and family, colleagues and neighbours; being active (go for a walk, do your exercises or some gardening, sing and dance!); be aware and take notice of the world around you, people and things, and consciously feel what you are experiencing; keep learning (try something new, or revive an old interest – challenge yourself!); and give something to others, a smile, a kind word, a cup of tea, a donation or voluntary service...

xvi   Humans are animals, and like other animals, naturally indulge in Habitual behaviour, follow the Herd, and seek the next 'High' – some pleasant, or at least convenient, experience. These three strong influencers often lead us astray: among other things, 'growing up' implies becoming aware of them, and learning how to control our own lives by making good choices, without (always) following the three Hs. In this regard good parents need to be both teachers and exemplars.

xvii   William Wordsworth's *Lines composed above Tintern Abbey*. He writes of 'feelings too / Of unremembered pleasure; such, perhaps, / As have no slight or trivial influence / On that best portion of a good man's life, / His little, nameless, unremembered acts / Of kindness and of love'.

xviii   Not all families conform to the traditional pattern. We see around us today many examples of 'blended', step, adoptive, mixed (like ours) or foster families. These poems are not judgmental, and nor am I. I hope they may provide help and support for every parent who reads them.

xix   Samuel Taylor Coleridge, *The Rime of the Ancient Mariner*: 'He went like one that hath been stunned, / And is of sense forlorn: / A sadder and a wiser man, / He rose the morrow morn.'

xx Our politicians and leaders refer to what they call 'the cycle of deprivation', whereby malfunctioning families seem to continue, generation after generation (in both senses!). But poverty is not the cause of incompetent parenting, though it is likely to be the result. Correlation is not the same as causation. What is certainly the case is that there are cycles of competent, and of incompetent, parents. The purpose of these verses is to reinforce the former, and help to transform the latter.

xxi John Bowlby, *Child Care and the Growth of Love*. He developed what he called 'attachment theory' and argued that the child's relationship to the mother in the first five years of life was critical. I am sure he was right. Since he wrote this book in 1953, seven decades ago, the world has changed in many ways, not least in family life and the practice of raising children. Governments in both developed and developing countries need women to join the employed workforce (to facilitate economic growth), and the feminist campaign to enable women 'to have it all' (see below, footnote xxvii), have each encouraged many mothers to 'outsource' childcare in the early years, sometimes even before the first birthday of the new baby. The question we all need to address is whether the alarming rise in mental distress in childhood (at present, rather unconvincingly, being explained by the period of 'lockdown' during the Covid pandemic of 2020), together with a range of conditions like acute anxiety, depression, eating disorders, ADHD, gender dysphoria, suicidal feelings and self-harm..., might be linked to the failure to establish secure mother-child bonding in the early years, as a result of the adoption of the 'kibbutz model' of child-care. The difficult lives of so many 'children in care' (and indeed 'late adoptions', of which we have some personal experience) might also, perhaps in large part, be due to the same cause. We need more research on this critical issue. Meanwhile, here in the UK, the government has announced in the 2023 Budget that it proposes to extend

free child care to parents of babies from nine months.
This sounds like a humane provision for those living in
relative poverty, but I doubt whether the young carers
will be adequately trained, properly supervised, or able to
provide the essential 'continuity of care that babies need.
I wonder how many babies each carer will be permitted to
take charge of at one time?

xxii *The Parenting Puzzle* was written for Family Links by
Candida Hunt and Annette Mountford. It is highly
recommended.

xxiii Samaritan volunteers make a commitment, when they
complete their initial training, to do a listening duty (of
about four hours) each week, *and* to attend one day's
'ongoing training' each year, without which they lose their
'licence to practise'. It is a good model for any worthwhile
enterprise, whether in the public, private or charitable
sectors – and also for parents!

xxiv This charming phrase describes the apprenticeship
model of learning, widely used in the vocational sector,
whereby the student learns by observing, assisting, and
practising the skills of the master of the craft. It works
best when good practice changes little over time (like
crochet, perhaps?), but is less effective when the craft, or
technology, or the society it serves, are changing rapidly –
as they are today. The question is whether parenthood is
more like crochet, or brain science?

xxv Google www.familylinks.org.uk training@familylinks.org.
uk or telephone 01865 401800.

xxvi While it is obviously true that single-parent families
will be disadvantaged by the loss (or desertion) of the
father, the evidence suggests that relative poverty is not
the only outcome. Our educational statistics reveal
that the children who leave schooling with the lowest
qualifications and the weakest entry-record to higher
education come from two racial groups: poor white and
black families. But, interestingly, if one disaggregates the
black families where the father came from Africa from

those where the father's origin was in the Caribbean, the former clearly outperform the latter. Responsible paternity is apparently more secure in African society than in the West Indies. It appears that, although racial differences still regrettably make a difference to children's chances (while the ability range in the two groups is, of course, similar), as we are all coming to recognise, the problem of the 'absent father' may be significantly responsible for the poor performance of both the children from the 'white under-class' and black children in families of Caribbean origin. Fathers matter. And marriage also matters: the Marriage Foundation has found that married parents remain united for a good deal longer than those who merely cohabit. And that is what children need, and want!

xxvii The practice of 'Working from Home' has been gradually increasing since the start of the century, but took a great leap forward during the years of the pandemic (2020-22). Of course, it isn't possible in some sectors of employment, like transport or retail, or professions, such as medicine and the law, although the social and technological changes of the future may prove this judgement premature. Nonetheless, it seems to offer us a model which might fully achieve the feminists' understandable (and reasonable) desire to 'have it all' (family, career, independent income – and sufficient time for this rich agenda), as men have long enjoyed, without sacrificing their children to the career (or vice versa). I hope this may prove to be so.

xxviii I owe these five principles (which he calls *respect*, *patience*, *trust*, *containment*, and *kindness*) to Guy Shahar, whose inspirational book, *Transforming Autism*, is warmly recommended.

xxix My greatest fear is that by 'normalising' bad practice, particularly early years outsourcing of maternal care, single-parenthood, and absent fathers, we shall gradually create a culture of toxic childhood. Normalisation is an interesting ethical challenge. It is best expressed in a question: is it all right to do something which (when you do it) will cause no harm, because you are a moderate, sensible, and self-controlled person – when you know others (who are not) may be encouraged to behave likewise? I think not. Consider smoking, alcohol and drugs, for example, or infringing the speed limit when driving, or smacking errant children... Parents should set a good example, not only to their children, but also to each other. The introduction of seat-belts in vehicles and the abolition of smoking demonstrate how hard it is to eradicate bad practice, once it has become normal. Our children deserve, and need, something better than a toxic childhood to prepare them to deal with the increasingly toxic environment (and culture) we shall inevitably bequeath to them.

xxx   Among the many excellent books on the subject of parenthood, I particularly recommend *Families*, by Jane James (2021). She emphasises the importance of our feelings, intuition and creativity (as a corrective, perhaps, to my rather masculine obsession with ideas?) and explains the four 'universal systemic principles' of belonging, exchange (human interaction), place and time. I am sure she is right.

xxxi   Recommendation 11 of my report on the importance of early learning (*Start Right*, Sir Christopher Ball [my alter ego], RSA, 1994) proposed that 'The RSA and other bodies should pursue the issues of: the education and support of parents, paid parental leave, and the care of pre-school children of those in employment'. Although much has been written and spoken in the past thirty years, I have come to feel that the urgency and force of this recommendation has still not received an adequate response. These poems reflect my own lifetime's study and learning of the arts and science of good parental care. If they do no more than help to stimulate the debate which is needed, to enable us to do the very best for our children, both at home and in the educational profession, in Britain and across the world, now and into the future, they will have served their purpose. The subject is so complex, good parenthood so challenging, and social change so evident, that the last word on this topic will never be written – least of all here! Nevertheless, those interested might peruse the *Start Right* Report (1994) and *Early Childhood Education Redefined* (Reflections and Recommendations on the Impact of Start Right) edd. Pat Preedy, Kay Sanderson and Sir Christopher Ball (Routledge, 2019) and consider the three key questions in the concluding chapter of the latter: 1. What are the essential qualities of the competent parent? 2. How may we ensure that everyone who chooses parenthood (or has it thrust upon them) develops and sustains these qualities? 3. What does good practice look like? (The acronym NESTLED offers a starting point.) These poems seek to explore good answers to the first and third question. Governments and societies, and parents the world over, need to address the second – for the sake of the well-being of future generations.